Contents

ISBN 0-634-00860-9

HAL•LEONARD®
CORPORATION
7777 W. BLUEMOUND RD. P.O. BOX 13819 MILWAUKEE, WI 53213

Visit Hal Leonard Online at
www.halleonard.com

BEVERLY HILLS 90210

(Main Theme)

from the Television Series BEVERLY HILLS 90210

By JOHN E. DAVIS

THEME FROM "COACH"
from the Television Series

By JOHN MORRIS

March tempo (in 2)

6

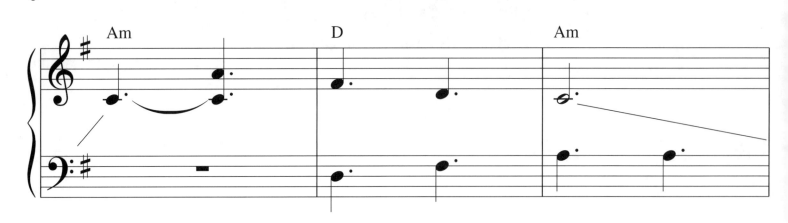

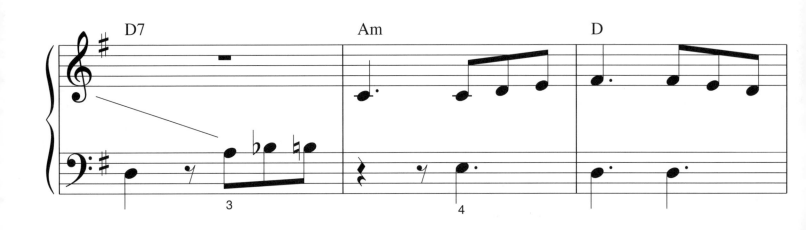

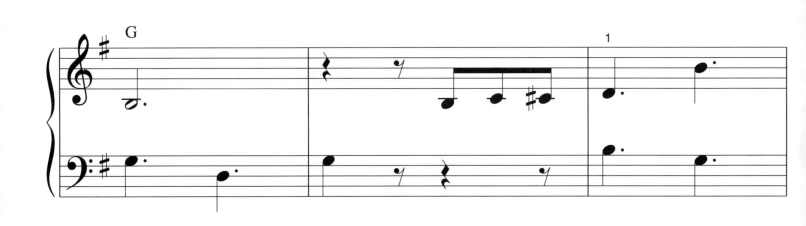

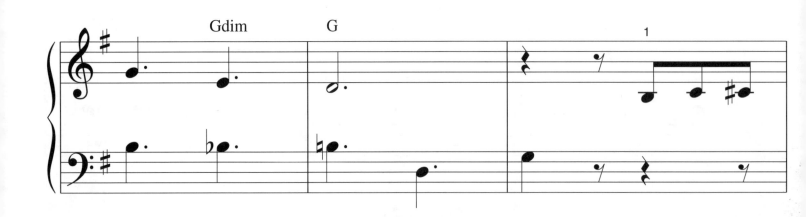

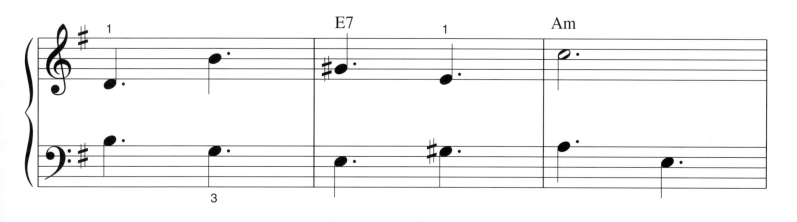

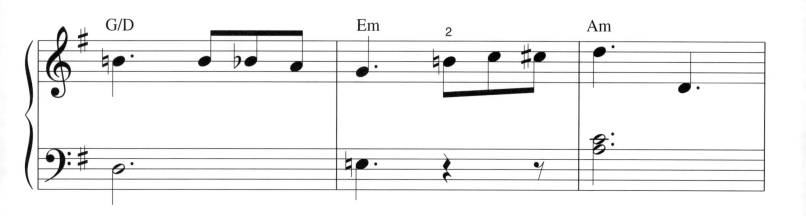

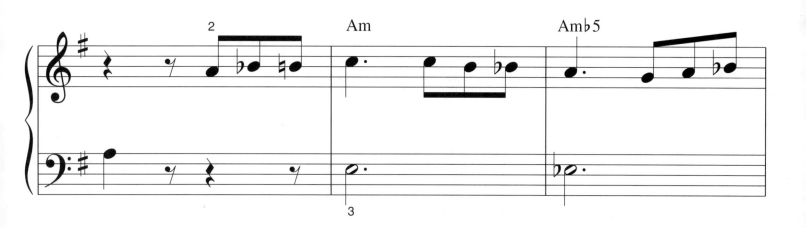

CLOSER TO FREE
from PARTY OF FIVE

Words and Music by SAM LLANAS
and KURT NEUMANN

Driving Rock

yeah, clos - er _____ to free,

clos - er _____ to

free.

COME ON GET HAPPY
Theme from THE PARTRIDGE FAMILY

Words and Music by WES FARRELL
and DANNY JANSSEN

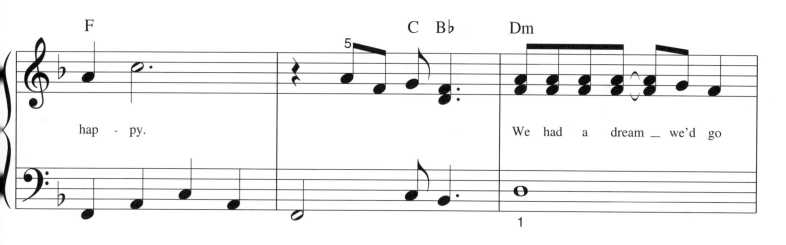

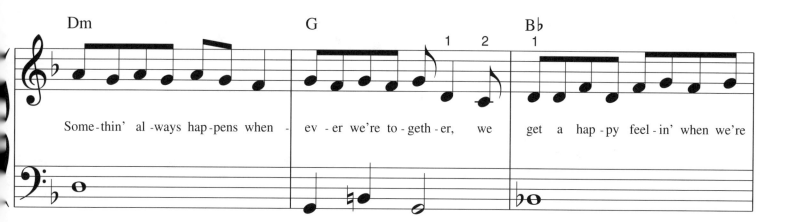

GEORGIA ON MY MIND
from the Television Series DESIGNING WOMEN

Words by STUART GORRELL
Music by HOAGY CARMICHAEL

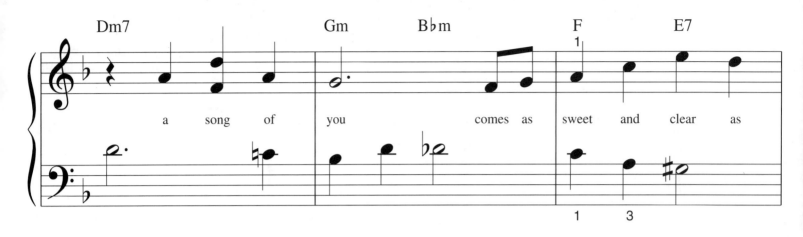

a song of you comes as sweet and clear as

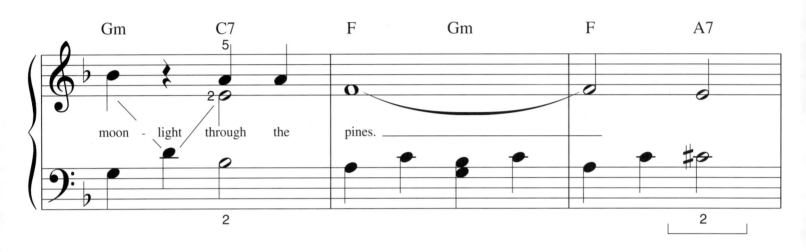

moon - light through the pines. _____

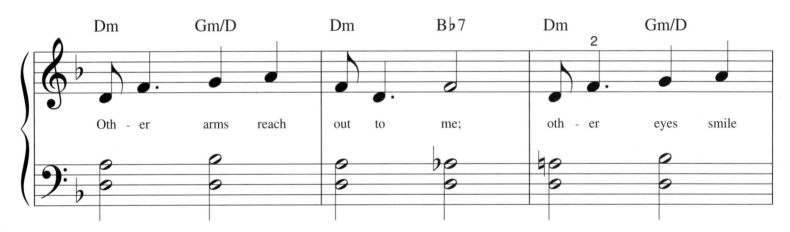

Oth - er arms reach out to me; oth - er eyes smile

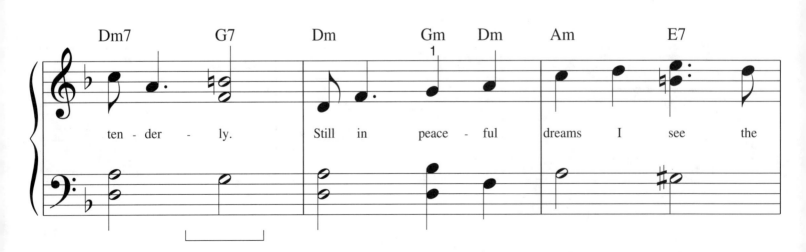

ten - der - ly. Still in peace - ful dreams I see the

COURTSHIP
OF EDDIE'S FATHER
from the Television Series

Words and Music by
HARRY NILSSON

THEME FROM "FRASIER"

from the Paramount Television Series FRASIER

Words by DARRYL PHINNESSEE
Music by BRUCE MILLER

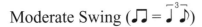

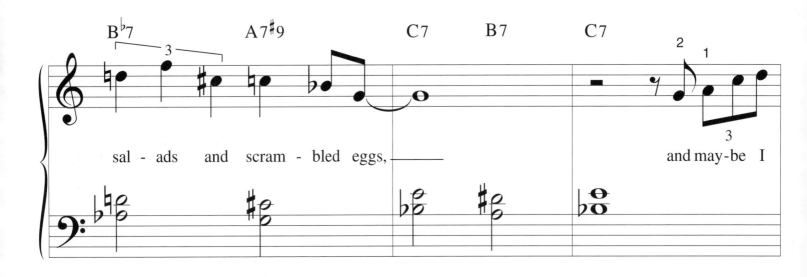

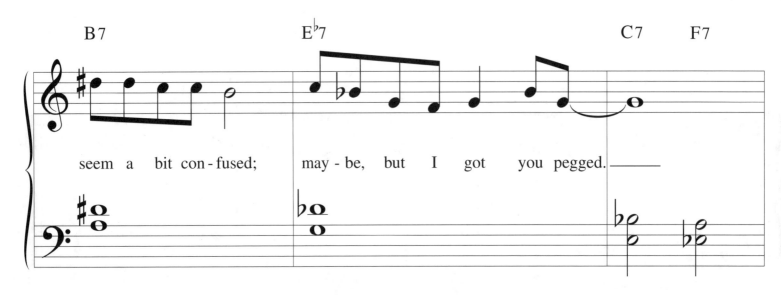

GET SMART
from the Television Series

By IRVING SZATHMARY

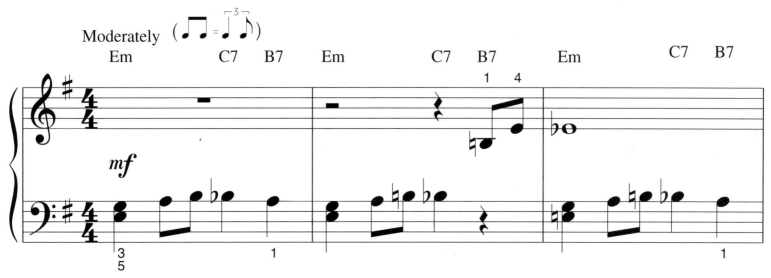

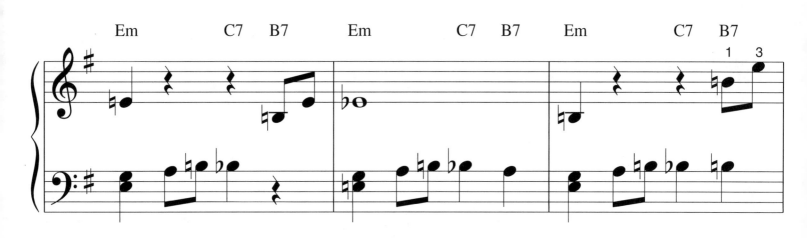

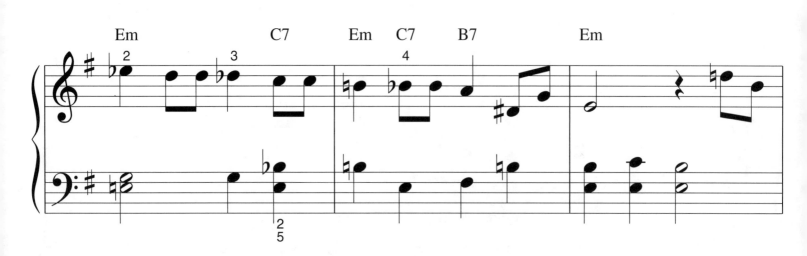

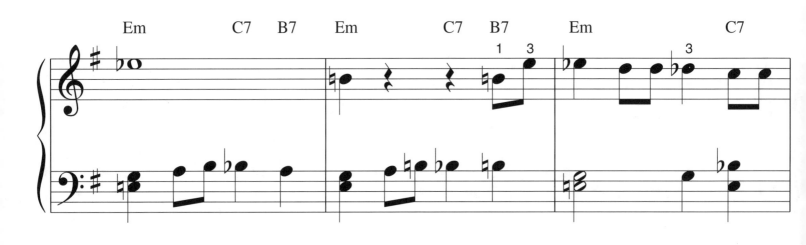

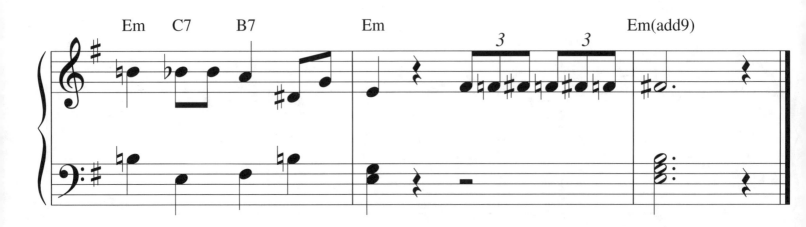

I DON'T WANT TO WAIT

featured in DAWSON'S CREEK

Words and Music by
PAULA COLE

Strongly

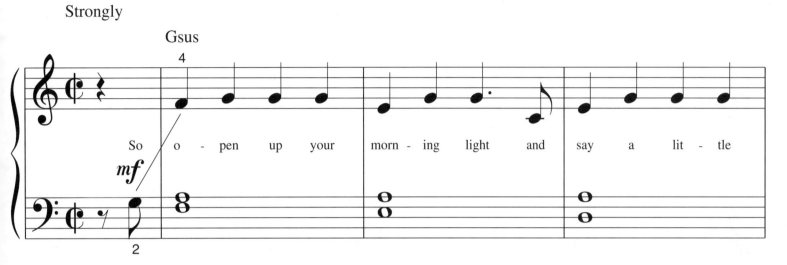

So o - pen up your morn - ing light and say a lit - tle

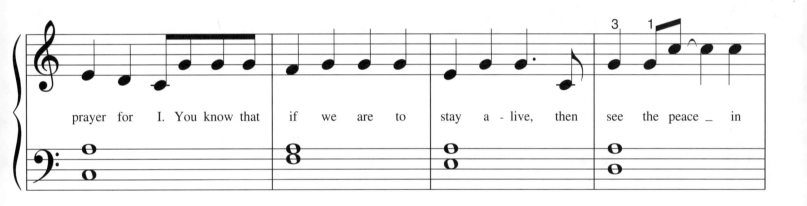

prayer for I. You know that if we are to stay a - live, then see the peace _ in

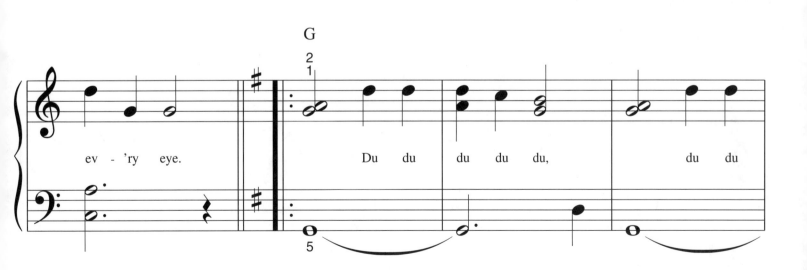

ev - 'ry eye. Du du du du du, du du

du du du,   du du   du du du   du. ____

She had   two ba - bies,   one was
He showed   up all wet   on the

six months, one was three,   in the   war of for - ty - four. ____
on the rain - y front step   wear - ing   shrap-nel in his skin. ____

Ev - 'ry   tel - e - phone ring,   ev - 'ry
And the   war he saw   lives in -

G/B   Dsus/A   Dsus   G

now, what will it be?   I don't want to wait

Em7   Dsus   C

for our lives to be o - ver. _____ Will it be yes, or

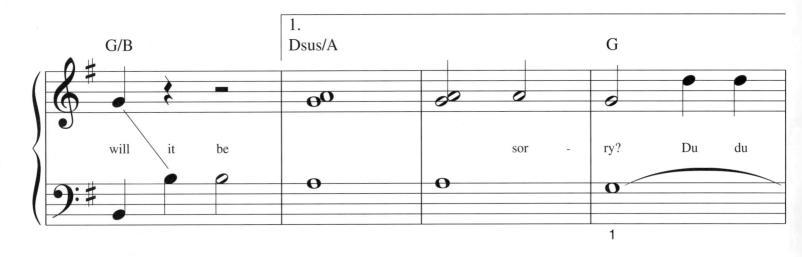

1.
G/B   Dsus/A   G

will it be   sor - ry? Du du

C

du du du,   du du du du du,   du du

HAPPY TRAILS
from the Television Series THE ROY ROGERS SHOW

Words and Music by
DALE EVANS

HARLEM NOCTURNE

featured in the Television Series MIKE HAMMER

Music by EARLE HAGEN
Words by DICK ROGERS

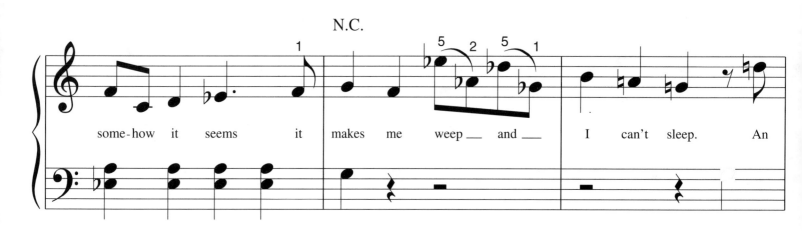

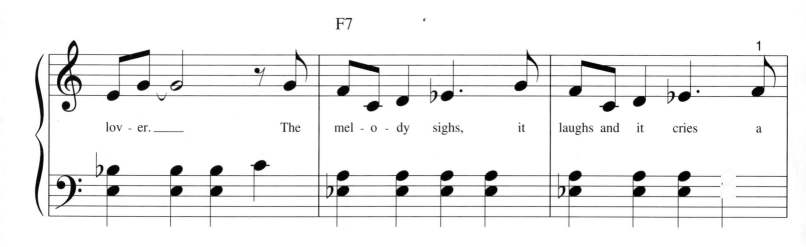

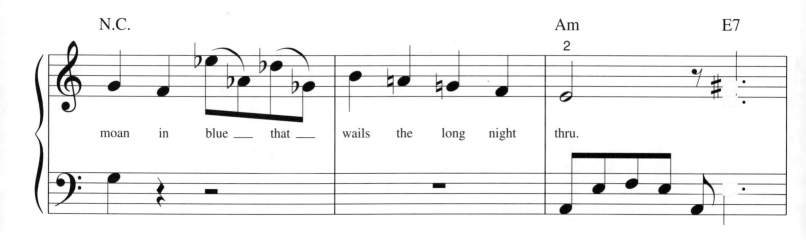

JEANNIE
Theme from I DREAM OF JEANNIE

By HUGH MONTENEGRO
and BUDDY KAYE

Moderately

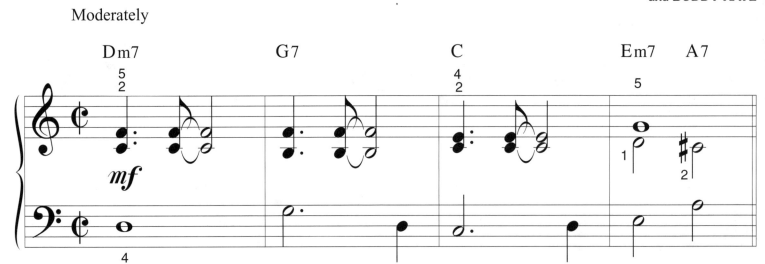

Jean - nie,——— fresh as a dai - sy! Just love——— how she o-beys me,

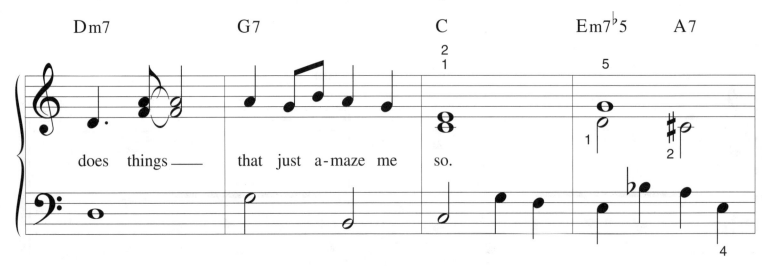

does things——— that just a-maze me so.

Dm7 — She smiles. — G7 — Pres - to the rain goes. — C — She blinks. —

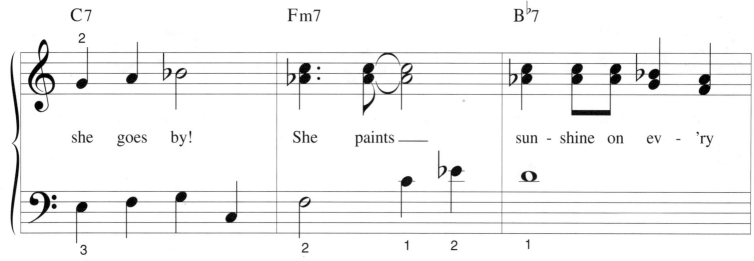

C#dim Dm7 — Up come the rain - bows! Cars stop, — G7 — e - ven the train goes — C — slow when

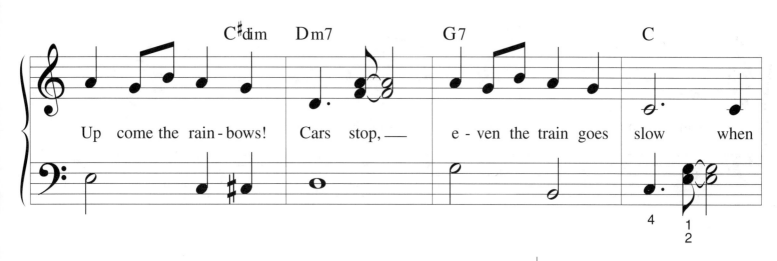

C7 — she goes by! Fm7 — She paints — Bb7 — sun - shine on ev - 'ry

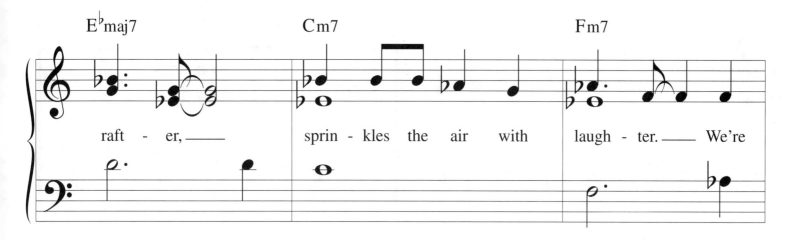

Ebmaj7 — raft - er, — Cm7 — sprin - kles the air with Fm7 — laugh - ter. — We're

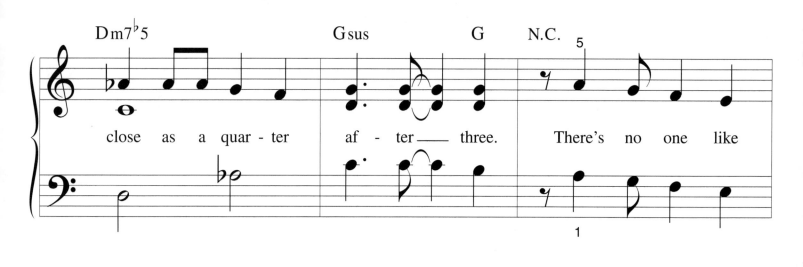

Dm7♭5 · Gsus · G · N.C.

close as a quar - ter af - ter —— three. There's no one like

Dm7 · G7 · C

Jean - nie. —— I'll in - tro - duce her to you, ——

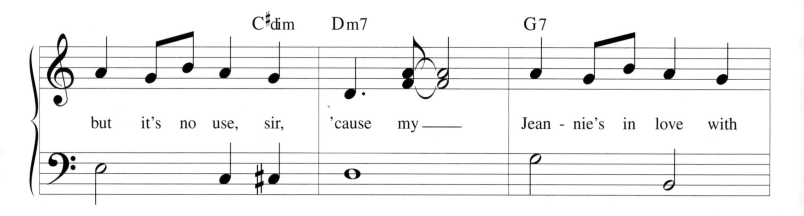

C♯dim · Dm7 · G7

but it's no use, sir, 'cause my —— Jean - nie's in love with

1. C

me!

2. C · B♭ · B · C

me! She's in love with me!

THE LIBERTY BELL
from MONTY PYTHON'S FLYING CIRCUS

By JOHN PHILIP SOUSA

Moderate March (in 2)

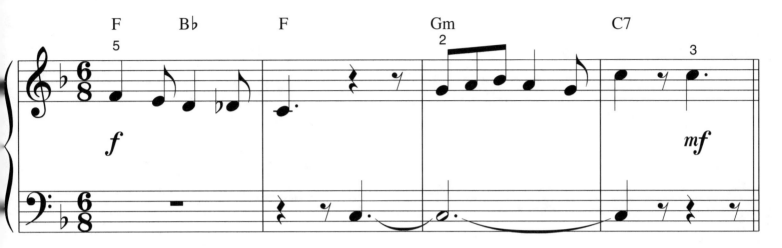

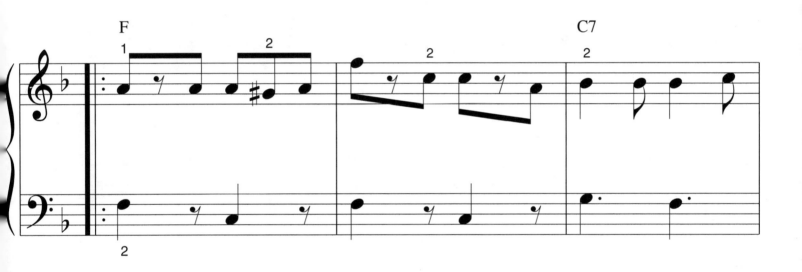

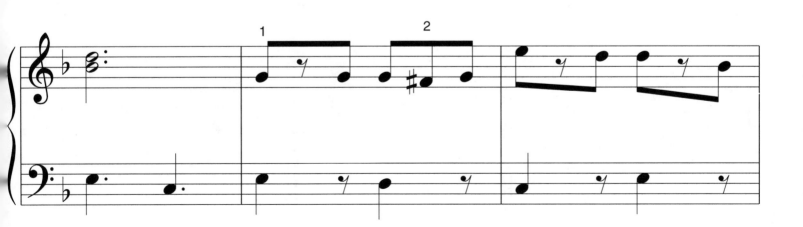

THE LITTLE HOUSE
(On the Prairie)
Theme from the TV Series

Music by DAVID ROSE

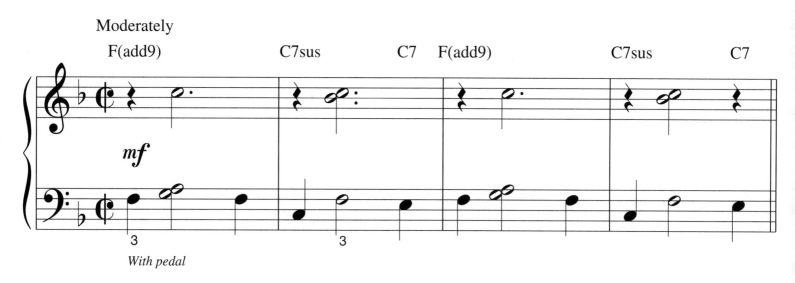

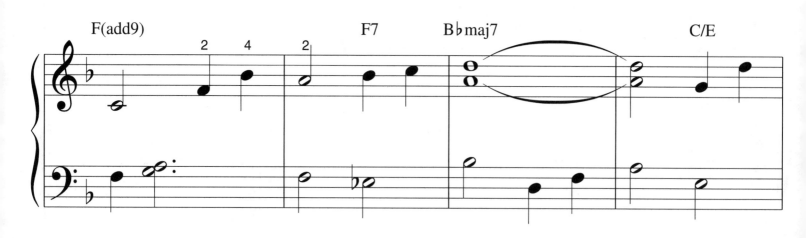

MURDER, SHE WROTE

Theme from the Universal Television Series MURDER, SHE WROTE

Music by JOHN ADDISON

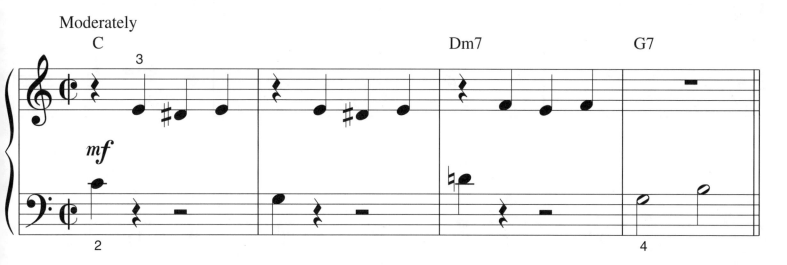

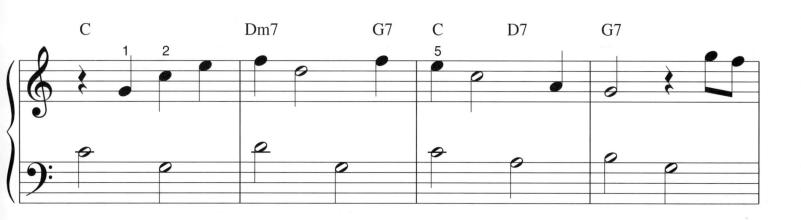

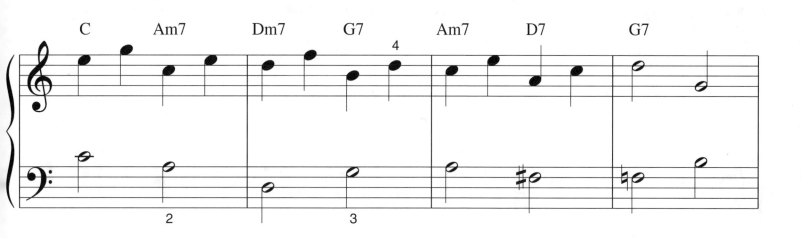

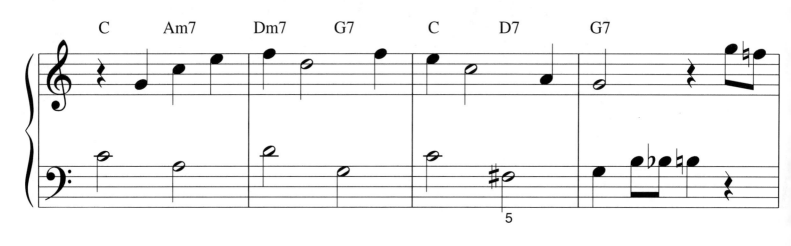

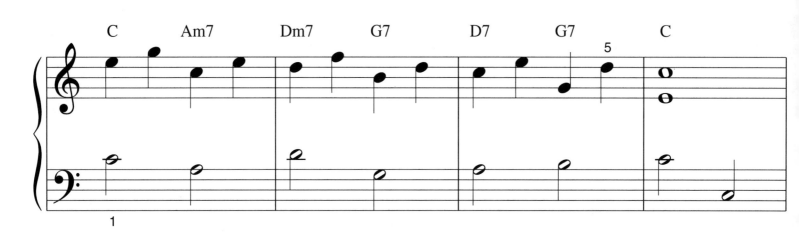

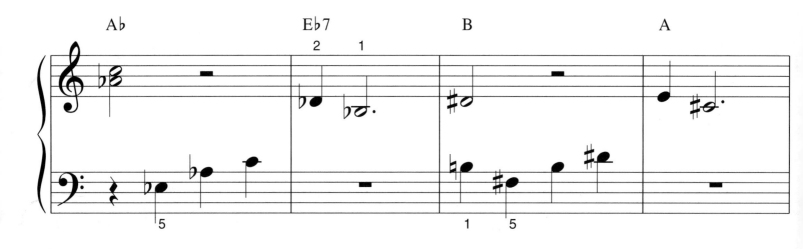

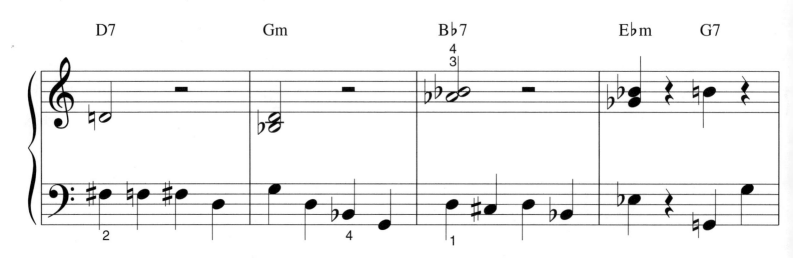

LOVE BOAT THEME

from the Television Series

Words and Music by CHARLES FOX
and PAUL WILLIAMS

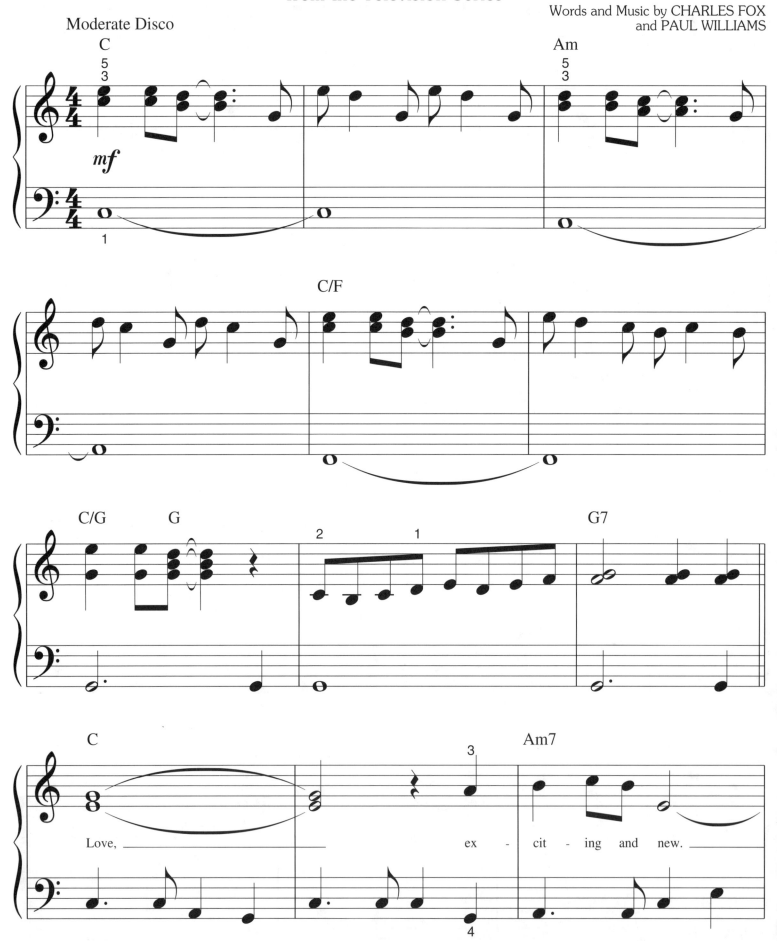

52

53

THEME FROM "MAGNUM, P.I."

from the Universal Television Series MAGNUM, P.I.

By MIKE POST
and PETE CARPENTER

MCA Music Publishing

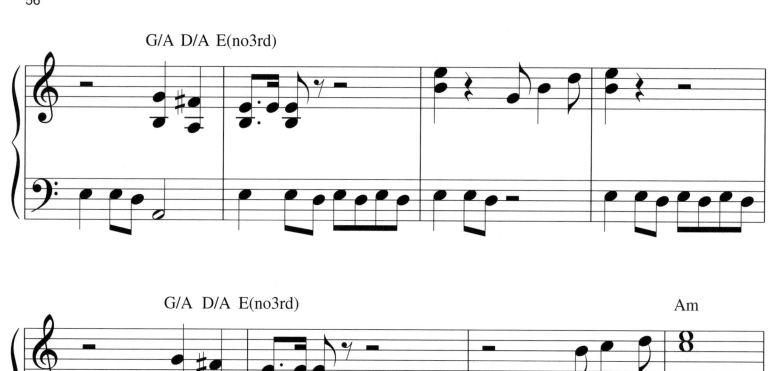

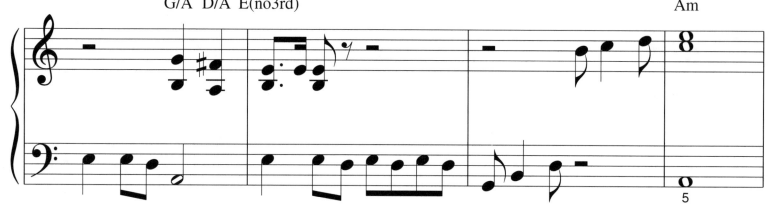

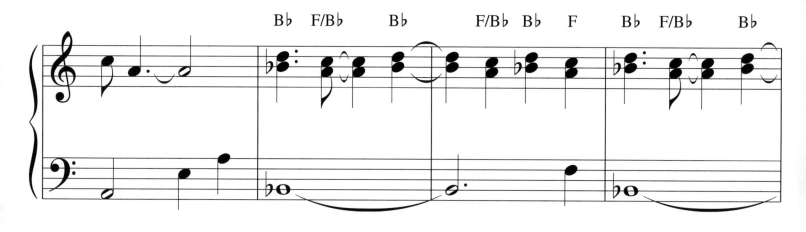

MELROSE PLACE THEME
from the Television Series MELROSE PLACE

By TIM TRUMAN

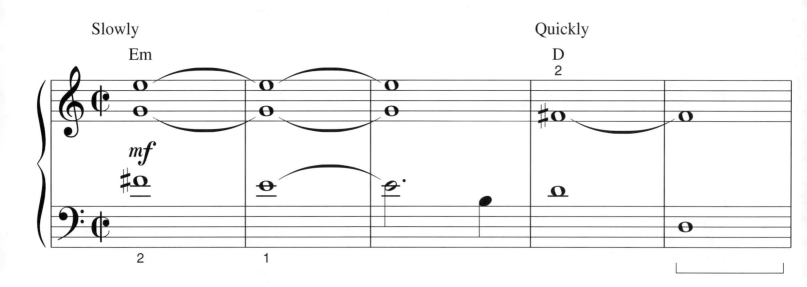

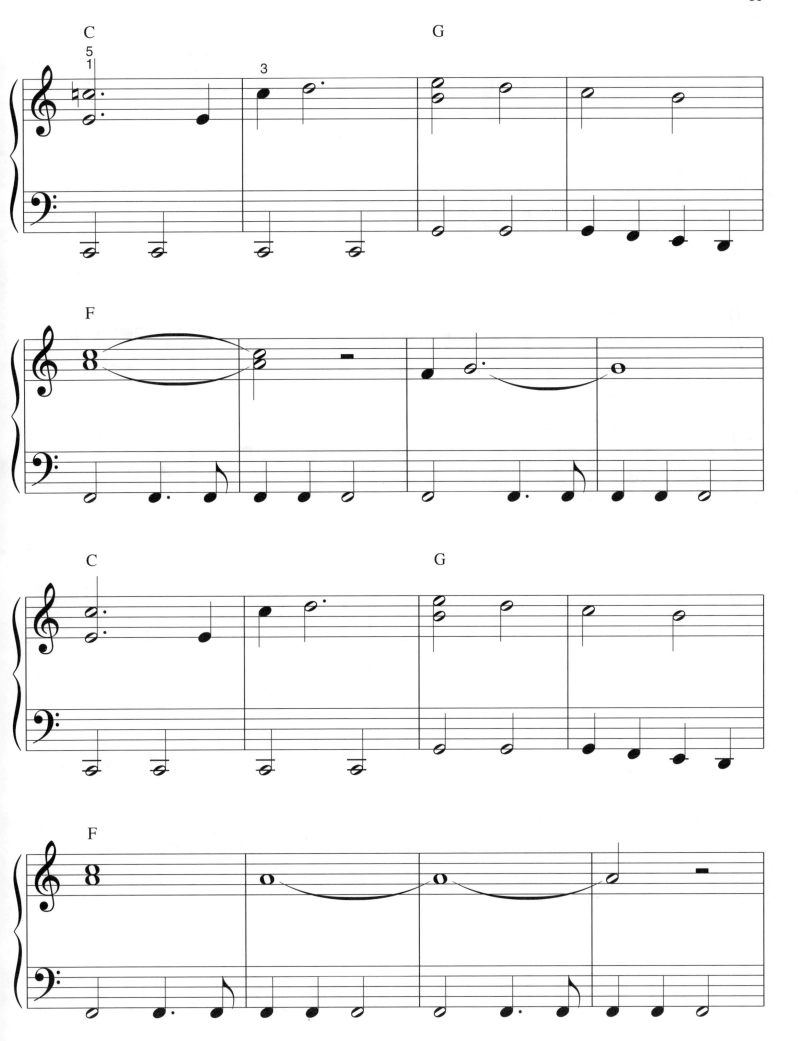

MICKEY MOUSE MARCH

from Walt Disney's THE MICKEY MOUSE CLUB

Words and Music by
JIMMIE DODD

63

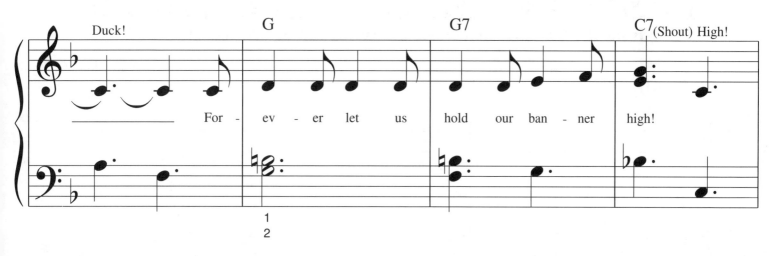

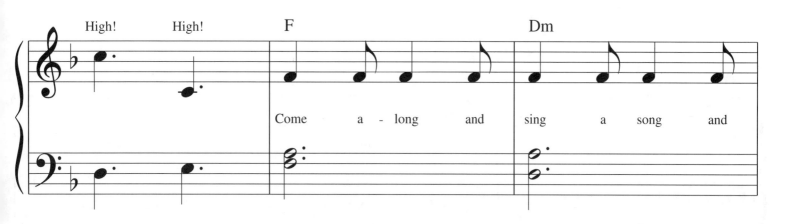

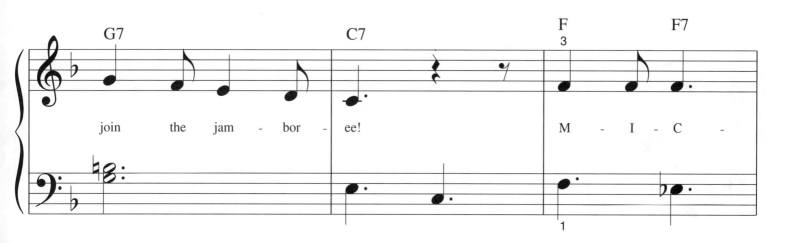

MISSION: IMPOSSIBLE THEME
from the Paramount Television Series MISSION: IMPOSSIBLE

By LALO SCHIFRIN

Moderately, with drive

NADIA'S THEME
from THE YOUNG AND THE RESTLESS

By BARRY DeVORZON
and PERRY BOTKIN, JR.

NATIONAL GEOGRAPHIC THEME
from the Television Series

By ELMER BERNSTEIN

Moderately

N.C.

THE ROCKFORD FILES
Theme from the Universal Television Series THE ROCKFORD FILES

Music by MIKE POST
and PETE CARPENTER

MCA Music Publishing

SOLID GOLD
Theme from the Television Series SOLID GOLD

Words by DEAN PITCHFORD
Music by MICHAEL K. MILLER

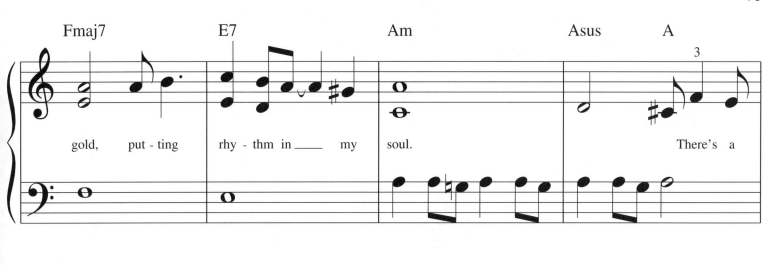

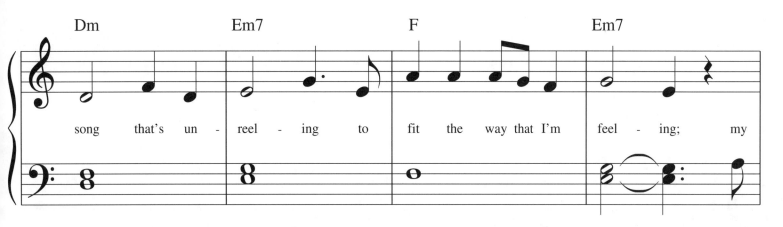

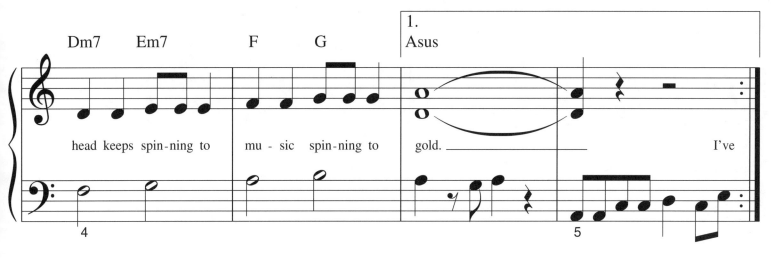

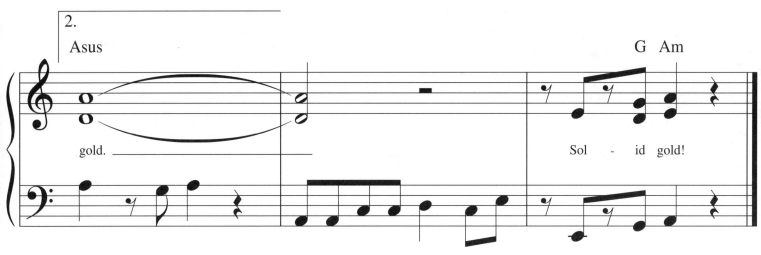

SAVED BY THE BELL
from the Television Series

Words and Music by
SCOTT GALE

Brightly

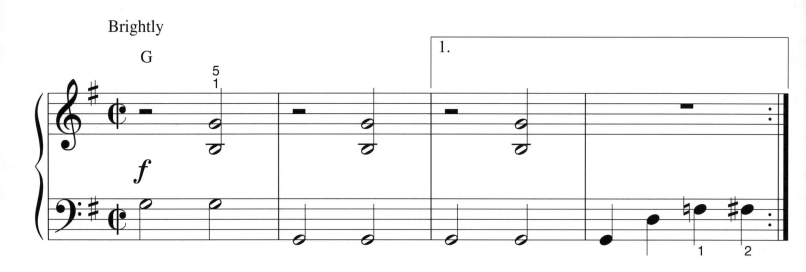

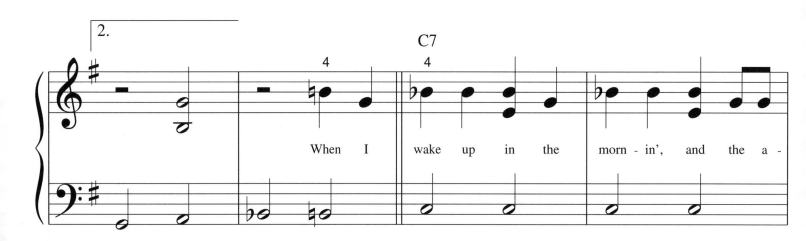

When I wake up in the morn - in', and the a -

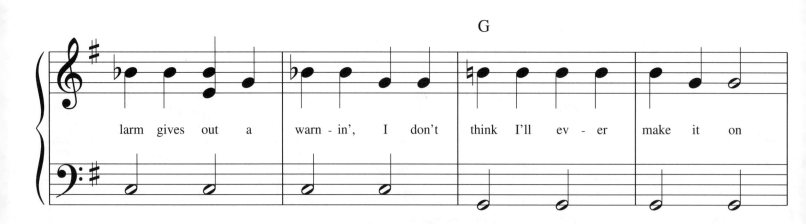

larm gives out a warn - in', I don't think I'll ev - er make it on

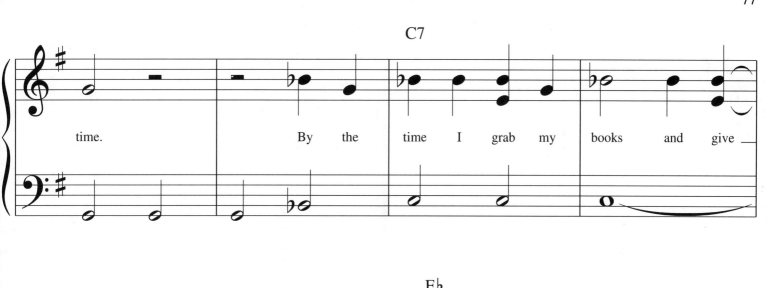

C7

time.   By the time I grab my books and give

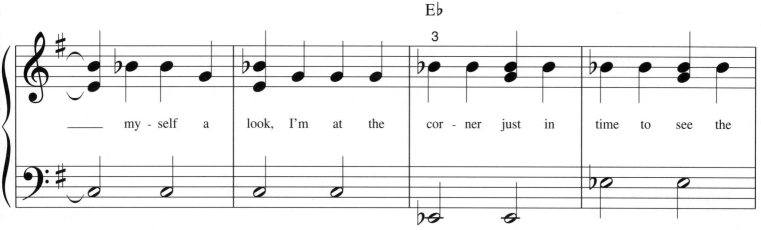

Eb

_____ my-self a look, I'm at the cor-ner just in time to see the

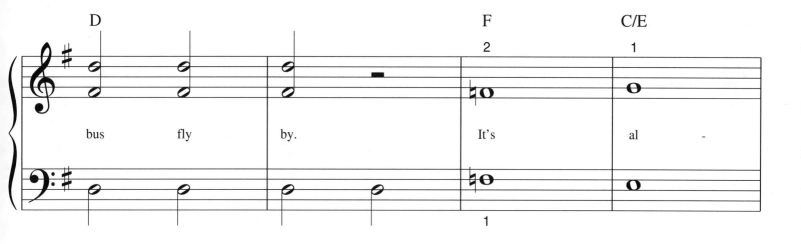

D   F   C/E

bus   fly   by.   It's   al -

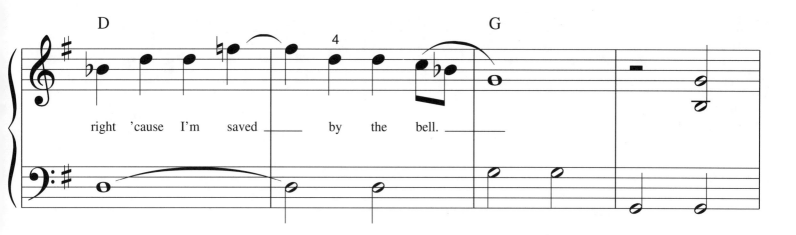

D   G

right 'cause I'm saved _____ by the bell. _____

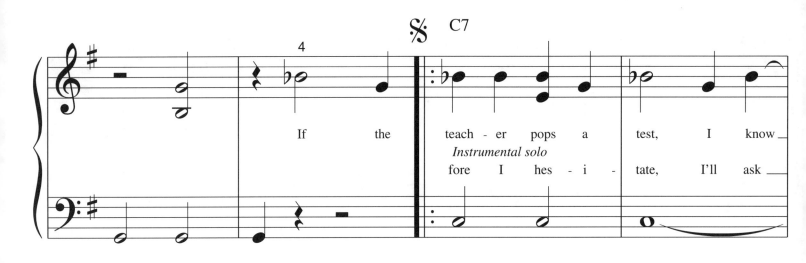

If the teach - er pops a test, I know _
Instrumental solo
fore I hes - i - tate, I'll ask _

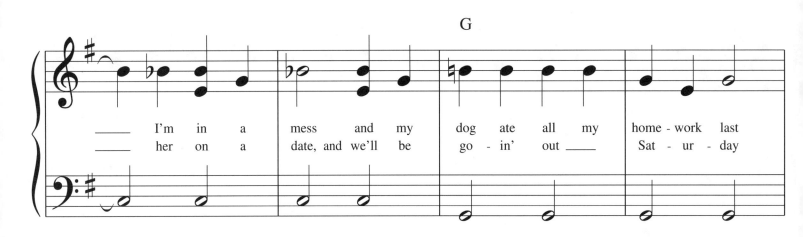

_ I'm in a mess and my dog ate all my home - work last
_ her on a date, and we'll be go - in' out _ Sat - ur - day

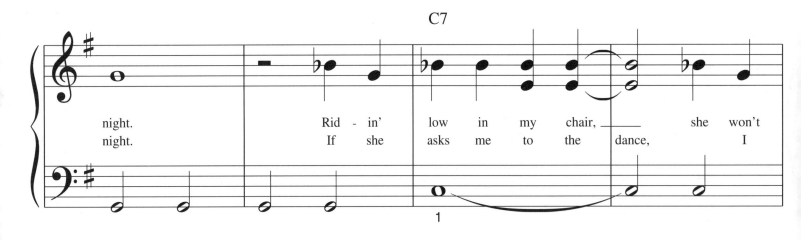

night. Rid - in' low in my chair, _ she won't
night. If she asks me to the dance, I

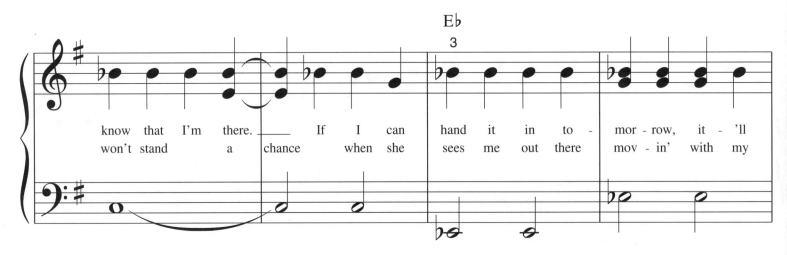

know that I'm there. _ If I can hand it in to - mor - row, it - 'll
won't stand a chance when she sees me out there mov - in' with my

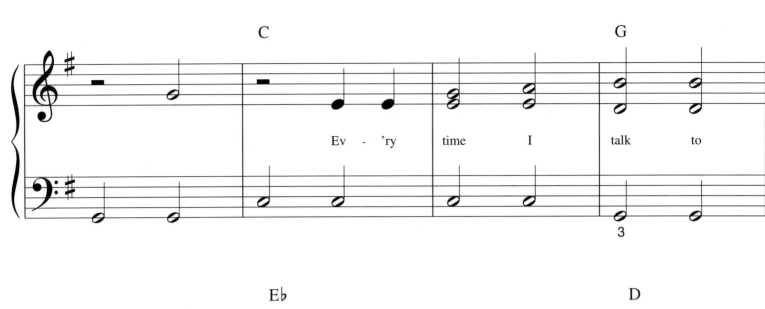

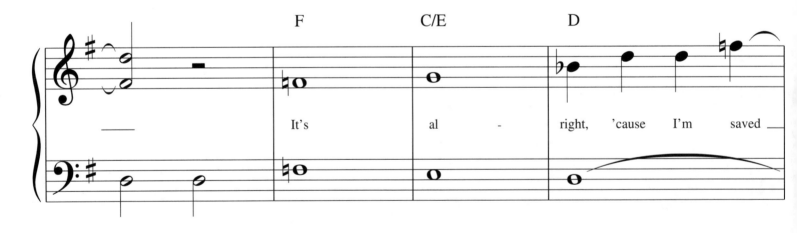

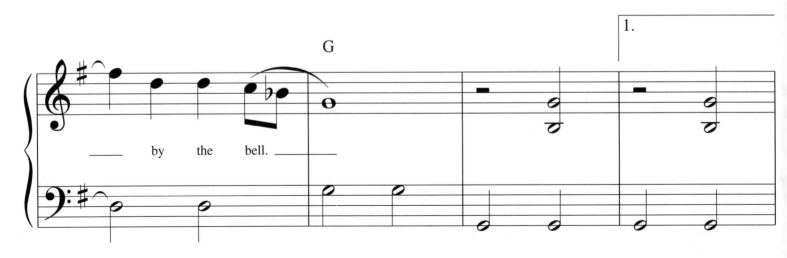

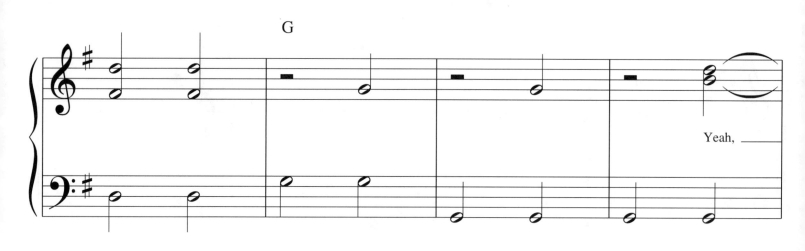

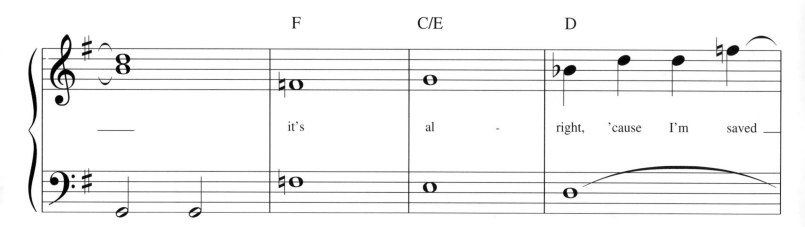

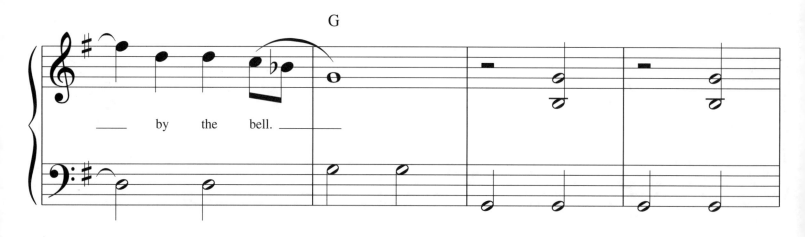

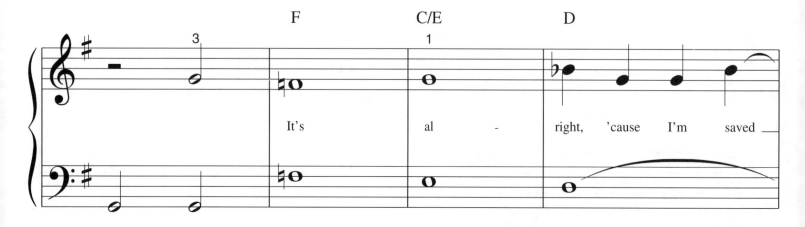

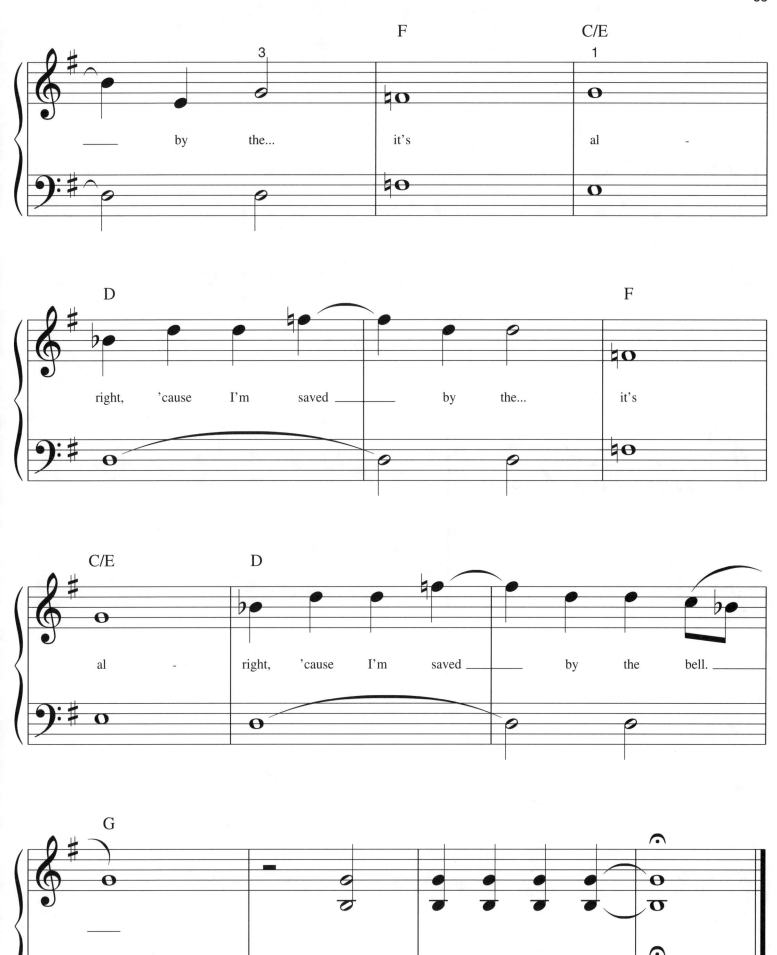

SECRET AGENT MAN
from the Television Series

Words and Music by P.F. SLOAN
and STEVE BARRI

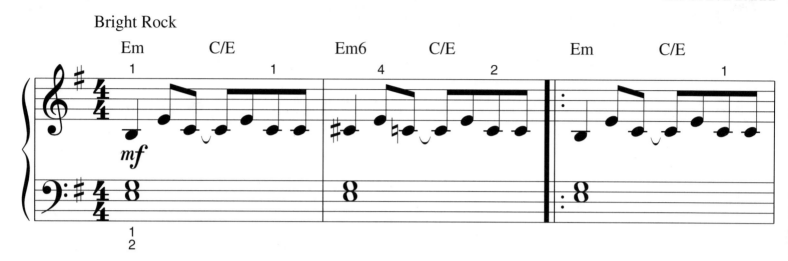

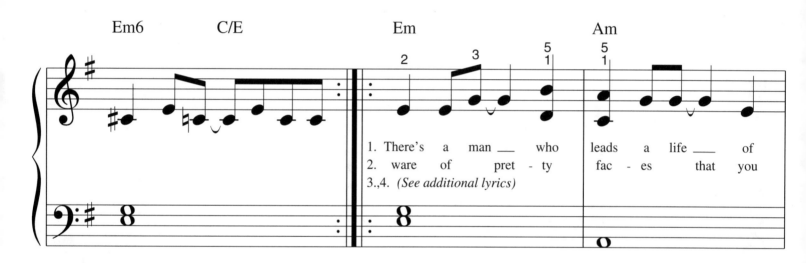

1. There's a man ___ who leads a life ___ of
2. ware of pret - ty fac - es that you
3.,4. (See additional lyrics)

dan - ger. ___   To ev - 'ry - one he
find. ___   A pret - ty face can

MCA Music Publishing

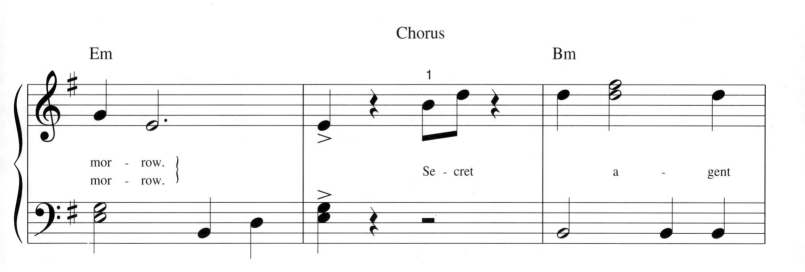

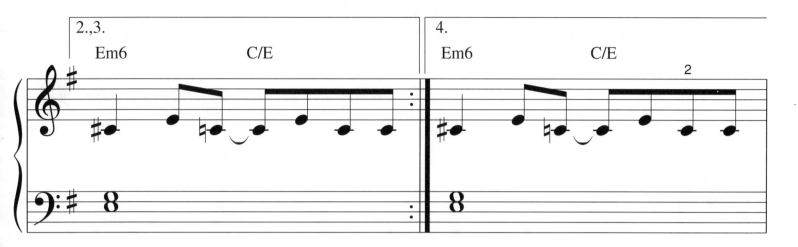

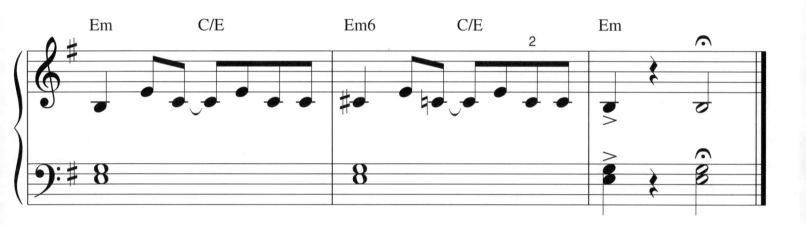

Additional Lyrics

3. *Instrumental*

4. Swinging on the Riviera one day.
   And then layin' in a Bombay alley next day.
   Oh, no, you let the wrong word slip
   While kissing persuasive lips.
   The odds are you won't live to see tomorrow.
   Chorus

WINGS
Theme from the Paramount Television Series WINGS

"Sonata In A" by FRANZ SCHUBERT
as Adapted and Arranged by ANTONY COOKE

Moderately slow

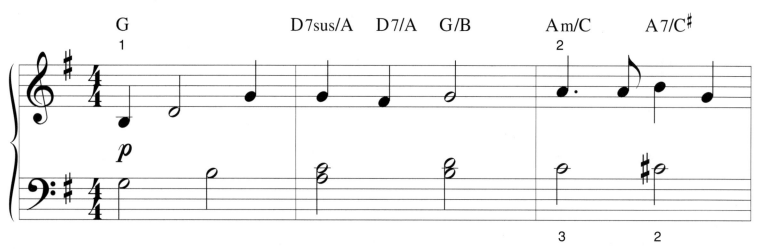

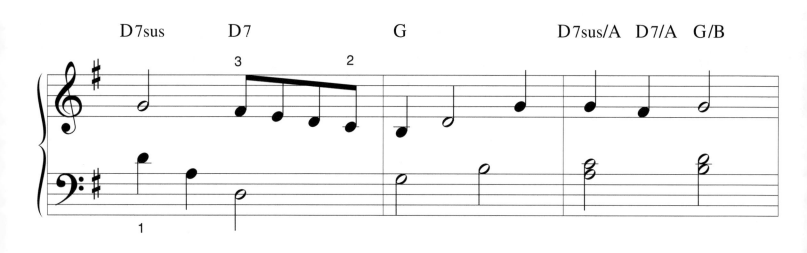

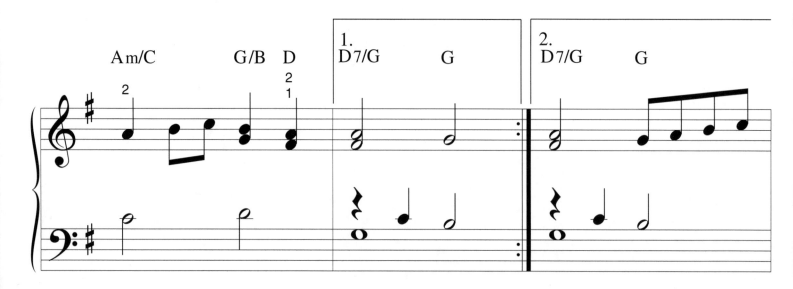

89

WITHOUT US

Theme from the Paramount Television Series FAMILY TIES

Words and Music by JEFF BARRY
and TOM SCOTT

Moderately slow

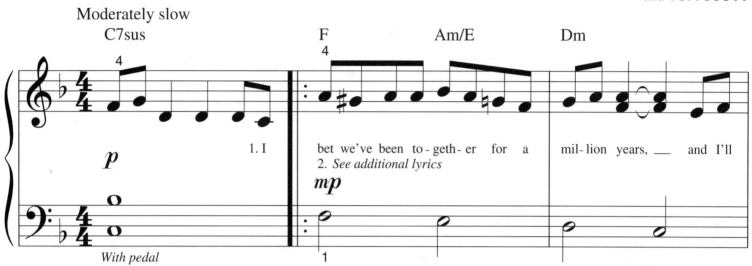

1. I bet we've been to-geth-er for a mil-lion years, ___ and I'll
2. *See additional lyrics*

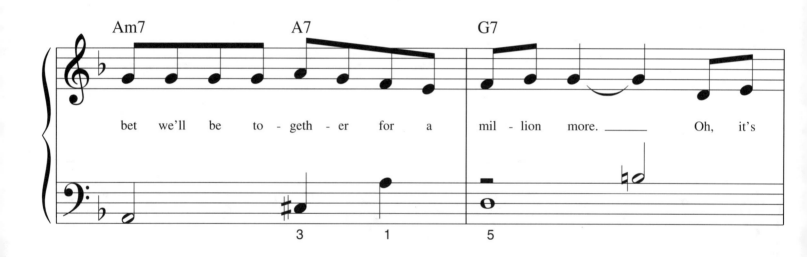

bet we'll be to-geth-er for a mil-lion more. ___ Oh, it's

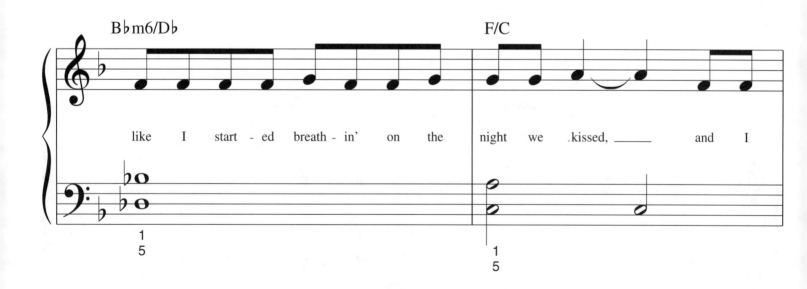

like I start-ed breath-in' on the night we .kissed, ___ and I

92

Additional Lyrics

2. If it's absolutely perfect,
   The last puzzle piece,
   And it all just comes together
   Like we had it planned,
   Oo, it's like we share a secret
   We could never tell.
   'Cause no one else but you and me
   Could ever understand.
   (To Chorus:)

STAR TREK-VOYAGER®

Theme from the Paramount Television Series STAR TREK: VOYAGER

Music by JERRY GOLDSMITH

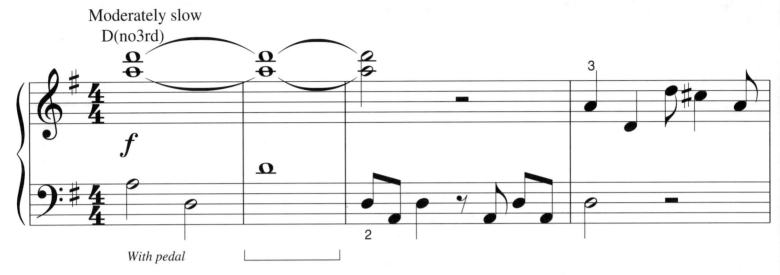

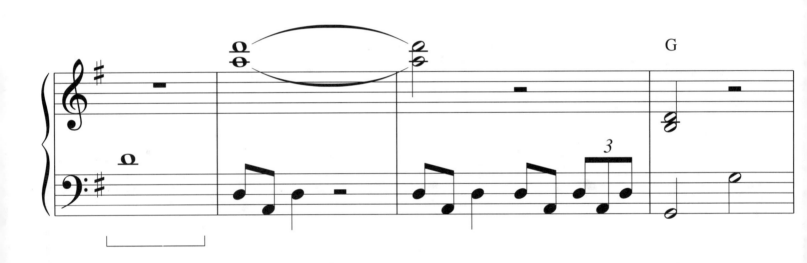

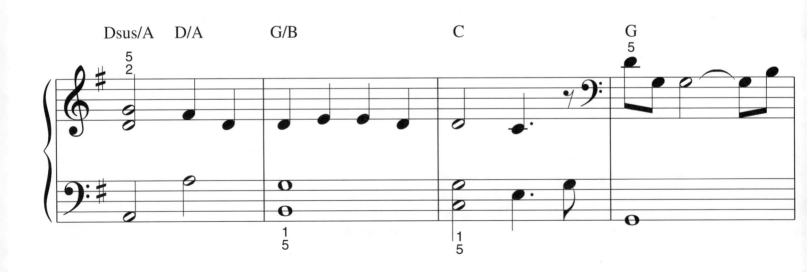